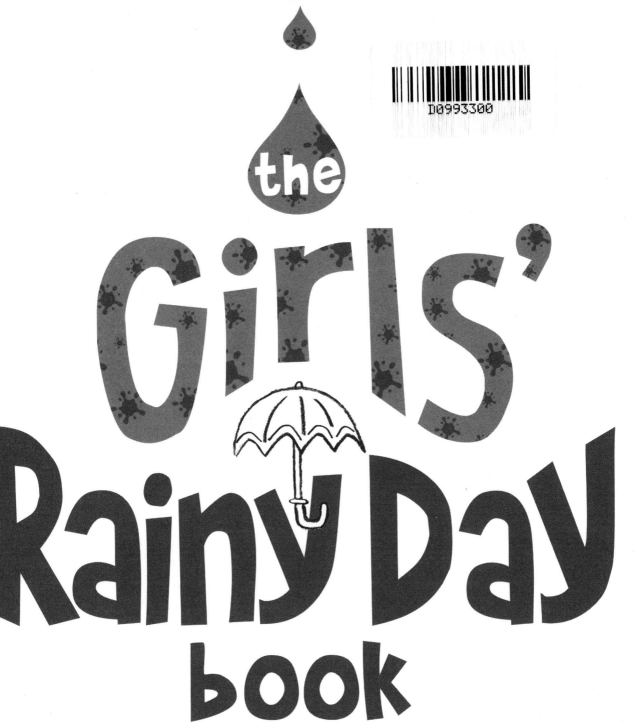

the Girls' Rainy Day book

Buster Books

Written by Ellen Bailey
Illustrated by Karen Donnelly
Edited by Elizabeth Scoggins
Designed by Barbara Ward
Cover illustrated by Andrew Geeson

The publisher and author disclaim, as far as is legally permissible, all liability for accidents, or injuries, or loss that may occur as a result of information or instructions given in this book. Use your best common sense at all times – always wear appropriate safety gear, be very careful with scissors, stay within the law and local rules, and be considerate of other people.

First published in Great Britain in 2011 by Buster Books,
an imprint of Michael O'Mara Books Limited,
9 Lion Yard, Tremadoc Road, London SW4 7NQ

A CIP catalogue record for this book is available from the British Library.

ISBN: 978-1-907151-30-9

2 4 6 8 10 9 7 5 3 1

www.mombooks.com/busterbooks

This book was printed in March 2011 at L.E.G.O., Viale dell'Industria 2, 36100, Vicenza, Italy.

Papers used by Michael O'Mara Books are natural, recyclable products made from wood grown in sustainable forests. The manufacturing processes conform to the environmental regulations of the country of origin.

CONTENTS

Decorate these girls' umbrellas.

GO FISH!

Go Fish! is a card game for two to five players – perfect for a rainy day when you and your friends can't go out.

HOW TO PLAY

1. All you need is a deck of ordinary playing cards. Start by dealing seven cards to each player.

2. Spread out the remaining cards, face down, on the floor or a table. This is your 'pond'. Each card is a 'fish'.

3. The aim of the game is to catch as many full sets of four fish as you can – for example, four twos, four eights, four kings and so on. The player to the left of the dealer goes first and asks one of the other players if they have any of the fish they are looking for:

'Katie, do you have any threes?'

4. If Katie has any of the requested cards, she must hand them over. If she doesn't have any, she tells the player to 'Go fish!' That player must then take a card from the pond.

5. Continue playing around the circle to the left, following steps **3** and **4**. When a player collects four fish of the same value, she places them face up in front of her on the floor or table.

6. If a player uses up all her cards on a turn, she fishes a card from the pond and play passes to the next player.

7. The game ends when all the cards have been used, and all the sets of four fish have been completed. Whoever has made the most full sets wins.

HOST A POP-STAR CONTEST

Are you ready for some all-singing, all-dancing fun?
Invite friends and family to join in as judges, performers
and audience members, and shine like a star.

Start by choosing the perfect place for performances – you'll need
a doorway for stylish entrances, a 'stage' area with plenty of
room for performers to show their best moves, and a space
opposite for the judges to sit. Don't forget to leave some
space for your audience.

BACKSTAGE PASSES

You also need a 'backstage' area for the performers to
prepare – your bedroom would be ideal. They will need
room to change into their costumes, mirrors to check
their star-style make-up, space to practise their moves,
and drinks and snacks to help them relax.

JUST JUDGING

Parents and grandparents make perfect contest judges.
Persuade up to four of them to join in, prepare a score sheet
for each person, with a column for each of the categories
shown below. Categories are scored out of ten, with a total
score out of 50:

Name	Styling	Singing	Dancing	Interview	Total

A WINNING PERFORMANCE!

To be sure of winning, contestants need to put on the best possible show for the judges. Here's how to get an outstanding score in each category:

Name:

Lots of well-known performers have stage names. For instance, Sandra Smith is a lovely name, but Sandrine Star is definitely a 10-out-of-10 superstar name. Come up with your own to really impress the judges.

Styling:

The judges must score each act on her overall costume – including her outfit, hair and make-up, if used. Try to choose outfits with as much sparkle as possible. Shiny fabrics will stand out particularly well. Add glittery make-up if you have any, and make your hair as gorgeous as possible.

Singing And Dancing:

Remember to choose a song you are familiar with, so you don't forget the words. Dance routines should be kept simple, so you don't get too out of breath to sing! The judges will still be wowed as long as you keep moving.

Interview:

The judges should ask each contestant a series of questions about her performance. Plan some answers in advance to avoid going blank, and remember to look the judges in the eye.

Top Tip. The judges should reveal the top three scores in reverse order for maximum suspense. The winner closes the contest with a final performance of her winning song.

RODEO ROUNDUP

Come on cowgirls! It's time to complete these challenges to win your very own indoor rodeo. You'll find the answers on page 62.

ROUND 'EM UP!

Which animal has each of these cowgirls lassoed?

MOST WANTED

One of the cowgirls is on the run from the sheriff – can you spot which one?

Sarah-Jane   Jessie   Lucie   Emmie   Katie

Goat
Calf   Bull   Pony   Prairie Dog

WANTED
FOR MAKING **FUN** OF THE SHERIFF

REWARD $500

Who's guilty? . . . .

LASSOSUDOKU

Complete the grid so that each row, each column and each block of four squares contains a boot, a hat, a horseshoe and a sheriff's badge.

WAGON BULL RUN

Run! Get away from the bull to the safety of the wagon. Can you find a route through the Wild West town that passes over just one cactus, one barrel and one tumbleweed?

Key: Cactus   Barrel   Tumbleweed

A MARIE-LOUISE MYSTERY

'The Marie-Louise is one of the world's great maritime mysteries,' Katie read to her brother Jack as they stepped on board the museum ship.

The ship was found abandoned in the Atlantic Ocean in 1864. It looked as though the crew had left suddenly, but there was no obvious reason why the crew would have left. The lifeboats hadn't been used, and there was no sign of a struggle. The Marie-Louise had been carrying a cargo of gold, and none of it was missing.

'Maybe they were kidnapped by pirates?' suggested Jack.

'It can't be pirates,' Katie replied. 'Pirates would've taken the gold.'

'Aliens then! Or a slimy sea monster!'

'There must be a good reason,' declared Katie. 'I'm going to explore below deck.' She headed down the rickety wooden stairs into the dark, damp coolness below and pushed open the door to a small cabin.

Inside, things were exactly as they had been when the ship was found without its crew in 1864. There was a small bed, a wardrobe full of beautiful dresses for a girl of around Katie's age, and a dressing table. *This must be where the captain's daughter slept*, Katie thought.

On the dressing table was a pretty coral comb. Katie knew this was a museum and that she shouldn't touch anything, but she couldn't resist and picked it up.

The comb felt cold and heavy in Katie's hand. She looked at herself in the mirror, just as the captain's daughter must have done all those years ago, and started to comb her hair. As the comb ran through the strands of her hair, Katie could hear music and singing from a long way away. As she continued to comb, it became louder and louder.

The room began to take on a greenish tinge, then vanished altogether. Katie found herself in another room entirely. When she heard a girl's voice chattering behind her, she spun around in surprise.

'A visitor! From above! Welcome, welcome – I'm Amelia. Did you use the comb? I suppose you must have done. No need to look so shocked. Although I was the same when it happened to me. Isn't it fantastic?'

Katie could hardly concentrate on what the excited girl was saying – for instead of legs, Amelia had ... a tail!

'Excuse me,' Katie said, 'but ... are you a mermaid?' She was half-alarmed and half-thrilled.

'Of course,' said Amelia. 'And so are you – look.' She

pointed down to where Katie's legs had been, to show her that she had become a mermaid, too!

'You've come to the most wonderful place – and your timing couldn't be better. We're having a party tonight to celebrate my brother's birthday.'

Amelia led her new friend through an underwater palace, stopping in every room to arrange displays of sea-flowers and shining shells. Katie tried to stop and admire the lovely coral walls of the palace, and all the pretty fish darting among them, but she had to swim fast to keep up.

As Amelia talked, Katie discovered that she was the daughter of the Marie-Louise's captain, and that it was because of her that the crew had abandoned the ship all those years ago. Amelia had found the comb hidden beneath the floorboards in her cabin. Her father had watched aghast as she had combed her hair with it and vanished. He had then instructed his entire crew to do the same, so that they could follow her and bring her back to safety.

When the crew discovered the land under the ocean, they loved it so much that none of them wanted to leave. Underwater, they would live for hundreds of years, and as the time passed, they forgot all about their lives above the ocean and their cargo of gold.

Finally, Amelia stopped talking and declared that it was time to get ready for the party. 'You need some jewels to match those beautiful blues and greens on your tail.' Katie smiled in delight as Amelia handed her a necklace of pearls and wove shells into her hair.

'It's all so magical!' Katie said to Amelia. 'But I can't stay. I left my brother behind, and my parents will be worried.'

Amelia sighed sadly. 'If you leave, you must always protect our secret,' she warned. Katie nodded, and a reluctant Amelia prised open a shell to release a second coral comb. She waved slowly as Katie combed her hair and vanished before her, returning to the ship.

The cabin door swung open and Jack poked his head around it. 'Have you solved the mystery yet?'

Katie quickly removed a piece of seaweed from her hair before her brother could see it. 'Not yet,' she said, as she took his arm and steered him out of the cabin.

HOW TO DRAW A MERMAID

Make the most of time spent indoors by creating your own picture of a beautiful mermaid. Here's how:

1. Start near the top of a fresh piece of paper, and draw a half-oval shape for your mermaid's face. Add a long wavy line to this, coming from the top-right of her head and down to the left.

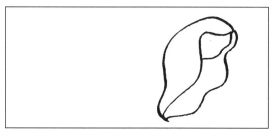

2. Build up your mermaid's hair by adding a long, curving line from the top-right of her head, down to the left, with a wide space between this and the first line. Then add a wavy line on the right-hand side of her face.

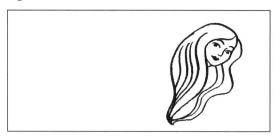

3. Fill out your mermaid's hair by drawing more wavy lines, as shown here. Then add her mouth, nose and eyes, trying to copy the shapes shown above as closely as you can.

4. To begin your mermaid's arms, draw two long lines coming out to the left and two shorter lines coming out from beneath her hair.

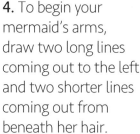

5. Copy the shape of the hands, as shown here, as closely as you can. Add the tail-shape by drawing two large S-shapes on the left, as shown above.

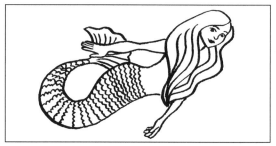

6. Now add a fan-shape to the end of the tail. Lastly, cover your mermaid's tail in small wiggly lines, like fish scales, to complete it. If you like, you can go over the lines of your finished drawing in black pen, before erasing the pencil lines. This will make it look really professional!

PUPPY POWER!

Can you work out which puppy belongs to which girl?
The answers are on page 62.

Rosie

Leila

Caitlin

A

B

C

DANCE AROUND THE WORLD

Can you match each dance style to its country of origin? Fill in your answers in the spaces below, then check to see if you are right on page 62.

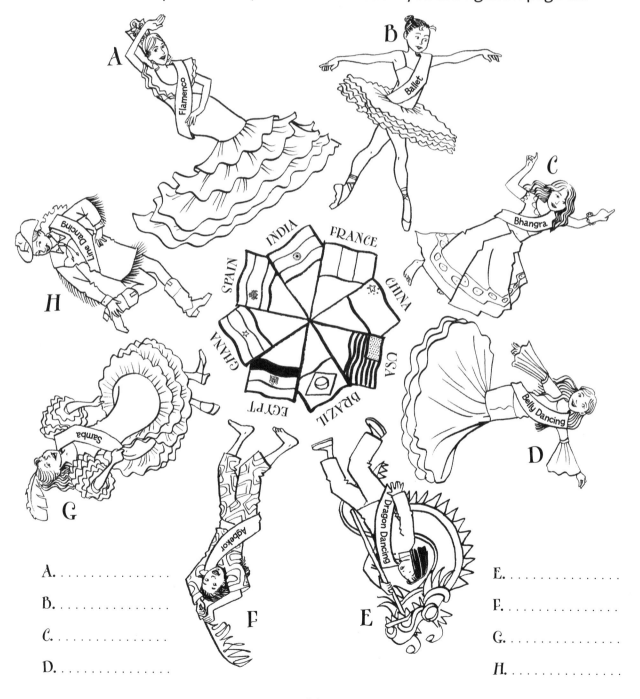

A. . . . .

B. . . . .

C. . . . .

D. . . . .

E. . . . .

F. . . . .

G. . . . .

H. . . . .

BUSY BEES

Busy Bees is a game for two players. Be the first to form a connected path of honey from one side of the hive to the other.

To play, you will need a red pen and a blue pen. Take it in turns to shade in any hexagon on the board below.

Player **A** must try to create a linked path from the top left to the bottom right of the hive. Player **B** must try to create a linked path from the top right to the bottom left of the hive.

SNEAKY BEES

You can use sneaky-bee tactics and use your turn to block your opponent.

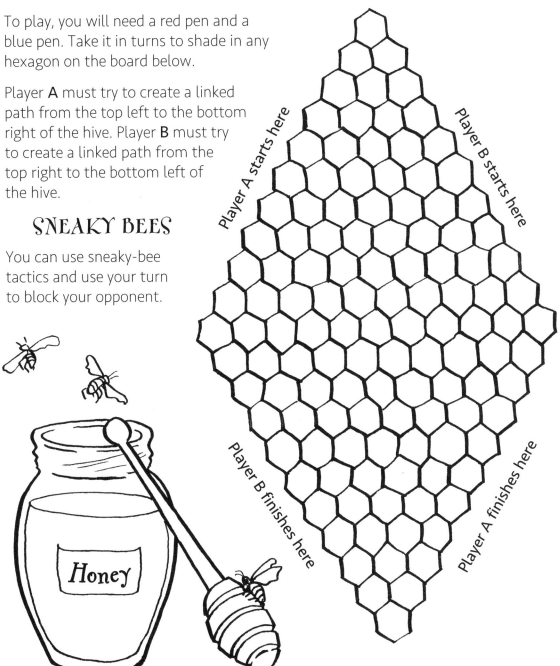

Player A starts here

Player B starts here

Player B finishes here

Player A finishes here

RELAX TO THE MAX

A rainy day is the perfect opportunity to wind down and de-stress. Spend some time looking after your mind and body with these relaxation techniques. Choose from the following, or make a day of it and do them all!

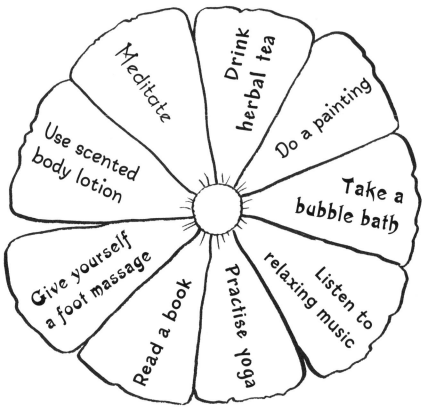

Meditate · Drink herbal tea · Do a painting · Use scented body lotion · Take a bubble bath · Give yourself a foot massage · Read a book · Practise yoga · Listen to relaxing music

MEDITATION STATION

Meditation is a great way to help you feel calmer and more relaxed. Here's how to get started:

1. Sit cross-legged on the floor.

2. Concentrate on your breathing and take ten long, deep breaths. When you breathe in, imagine peace and calm entering your body, and when you breathe out, imagine all the tension leaving your body.

3. Continue to breathe deeply and evenly, but now focus your mind on all the good things in your life. Think about the people you love and the things you enjoy doing. This will help you to feel calm, happy and full of energy.

4. Finish with five more long, deep breaths.

5. Write down any ideas or thoughts that came to you during your meditation in a notebook.

SIX-STEP YOGA

As well as making you feel more relaxed, yoga is a great way to stretch your muscles and to improve your flexibility. Try holding each pose in this series for a minute and see how you feel.

1. Lie flat on your back with your palms facing the ceiling.

2. Hug your knees to your chest.

3. Sit up and stretch your legs out in front of you. Place your hands on the floor at your sides. Gently bend your neck and tilt your head forwards towards your chest.

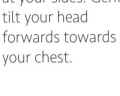

4. Stand up. Stretch your arms up above your head and press the palms of your hands together.

5. Raise one foot off the ground and rest it against the side of your other leg. Repeat with the other foot.

6. Lastly, shake your body out like this.

WHAT'S YOUR SOCIAL STYLE?

When wet weather strikes, what do your choices say about you?
Try out this quiz to discover the true you!

START

It's a rainy Saturday – what are you doing?

Calling on your friends to see who wants to put on their wellies and have some fun!

Which of these sets of activities would you choose?

Going on picnics, day trips and shopping expeditions with your friends.

You and your friends are planning a trip to a theme park – what's your role?

Spending hours with your friends chatting, daydreaming and flicking through magazines.

It's your birthday next week – what have you got planned?

Enjoying spending some time alone at home – it's so quiet and relaxing!

Tickets to something that you could go to together.

What is the best present you've ever given someone?

Something personal that you've spent hours making.

You're going on holiday tomorrow – what are you doing?

18

You're in charge of organizing everything and everyone.

You came up with the idea and got everyone excited about it – the details are up to someone else.

You're having all your friends over for dinner and a sleepover.

You've got lots of ideas and will make a spontaneous decision on the day.

Spending time with your best friend before you're separated – you can pack in the morning.

Double-checking that you've packed everything on your list.

LEADER OF THE PACK

You are full of energy and have a strong, passionate social style. Your friends love your ability to make things happen. You're ambitious and know your own mind.

SOCIAL BUTTERFLY

You find it easy to make new friends and have a confident and relaxed social style. You're easy-going, creative and fun to be around.

LAID-BACK LADY

You are caring, kind and have an accepting and affectionate social style. Your friends know they can depend on you always to be there for them.

SOPHISTICATED SISTER

You're a deep thinker and have a self-reliant, independent social style. You are happy spending time on your own and have a small group of very close friends.

PLAY THE CHESHIRE CAT

The Cheshire Cat is known for his mischievous grin, and getting people to smile is the aim of this game! Can you keep a straight face? Here's how to play:

1. A group of people sit in a circle with one person in the middle.

2. The person in the middle is the Cheshire Cat. Her job is to walk around on her hands and knees, purring and behaving like a cat in order to make the other players smile.

3. The Cheshire Cat should go up to each of the players in turn and say in a cat-like voice, 'Smile if you love me.'

The player must then respond, 'I do love you, Kitty, but I just can't smile.'

4. If any of the players smile at any point, whether she is talking to the Cheshire Cat or not, she becomes the Cat and must swap places with the person in the middle of the circle.

5. If none of the players smile, then the person in the middle continues going around asking everyone until she manages to get someone to smile.

PICTURE THIS!

Using the grid lines to help you, draw your own version of this picture in the bigger grid below, with pens or pencils.

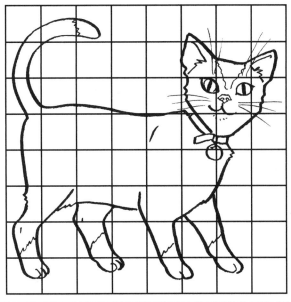

HAWAIIAN LUAU

Aloha! Let's party, Hawaiian-style! Once you've worked these puzzles out, check your answers on page 62.

You've been invited to a traditional Hawaiian luau party. Follow the instructions on the invitation to find your way there. Is the party at the Shark Cove Café, the Halona Blowhole or the Diamond Lighthouse?

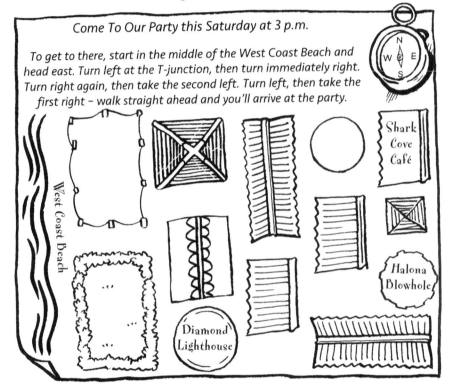

Come To Our Party this Saturday at 3 p.m.

To get to there, start in the middle of the West Coast Beach and head east. Turn left at the T-junction, then turn immediately right. Turn right again, then take the second left. Turn left, then take the first right – walk straight ahead and you'll arrive at the party.

West Coast Beach

Shark Cove Café

Halona Blowhole

Diamond Lighthouse

SUDOKU HAWAIIAN-STYLE

Complete the grid so that each row, each column and each outlined block of four squares contains only one heart, one turtle, one flower and one sun.

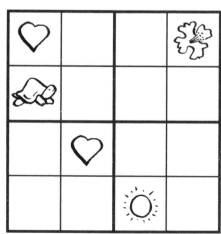

LUSCIOUS LUAU SMOOTHIES

Can you spot which of these tropical fruit smoothies is yours? The one you're looking for has a cocktail stick with at least one cherry on it. It has a cocktail umbrella and is in a tall glass, but does not have a straw.

PARADISE DIVIDE

Can you draw two straight lines across the beach to divide it into four areas? Each area must have one palm tree and one tiki torch in it.

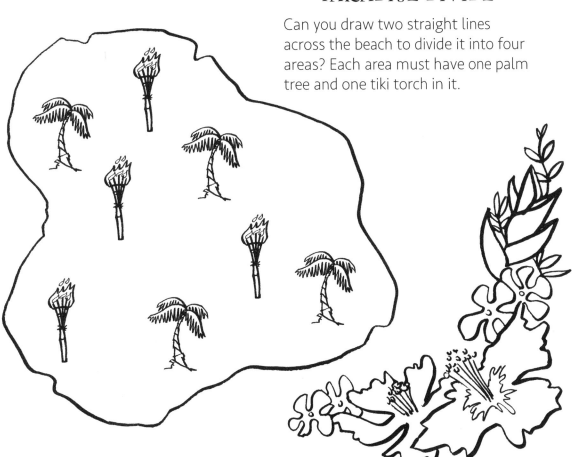

DESERT-ISLAND DESSERTS

Bring some sunshine to your day with these delicious desert-island cupcakes. No one would mind being stranded on one of these islands!

You will need:

• 100 g (½ cup) butter, at room temperature • 100 g (½ cup) caster sugar (superfine sugar) • 2 eggs • 100 g (1 cup) self-raising flour.

What you do:

1. Preheat the oven to 180 °C/350 °F/ Gas mark 4.

2. In a large bowl, beat the butter and sugar together using the back of a wooden spoon until the mixture is creamy and fluffy.

3. Crack one egg into the mix and stir it in thoroughly, then do the same with the other. Whisk until smooth.

4. Sift the flour into a separate bowl.

Warning: Always ask an adult to help you when you would like to use the oven.

5. Add the flour to the wet mixture a little at a time, using a metal spoon to gently 'fold' it in.

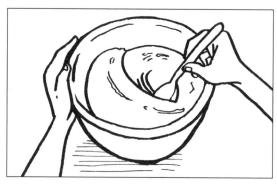

6. Place 12 cupcake cases (papers) in a bun tin (cupcake pan) and divide the cake mix evenly between them.

7. Bake for 20 minutes, or until lightly golden, and place on a wire rack to cool. Ask an adult to help you with this bit.

TRANSFORMING YOUR CUPCAKES INTO ISLANDS

You will need:

• 200 g (1 cup) butter, at room temperature • 400 g (4 cups) icing sugar (powdered sugar) • 4 tablespoons of milk • blue food dye • chopped nuts • fish-shaped jelly sweets, if available • chocolate fingers • green paper.

1. To make the topping, beat the butter with the back of a wooden spoon until it is soft, then gradually add the sugar. When you have beaten the sugar in, add the milk and mix thoroughly.

2. Ask an adult to check the cupcakes are cool and peel off the cases (papers).

3. If the cakes have risen a lot, use a dinner knife to cut across the tops, so they are flat. Turn them over and spread topping over what is now the top of each cupcake to make into little islands.

4. Add several drops of blue food dye to the remaining topping and mix thoroughly. Use this to cover the sides of the cakes to make the ocean.

5. Next, sprinkle chopped nuts over your islands, before the topping dries, to make pebbly beaches.

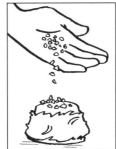

6. Push your fish-shaped sweets into the sides of the cupcakes, as though they are swimming in the ocean.

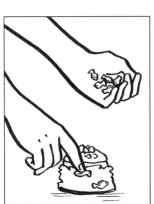

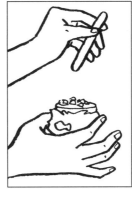

7. Gently push a chocolate finger into the middle of each desert island, so that they stand upright. These are the trunks of the palm trees.

8. Cut 36 leaves out of the green paper. Then use a dab of spare topping to stick each one to the top of the chocolate fingers (three per tree).

Enjoy your desert island dessert with friends!

Warning: Make sure you leave out the nuts if you or your friends or family have a nut allergy.

FRIENDOMETER

Each description below is worth a certain number of Friendship Points. Read each one, and, if the sentence describes you perfectly, you can shade in the number of points shown, starting from the bottom of your Friendometer. How close to the top can you get?

HOW GOOD A FRIEND ARE YOU?

• I don't get jealous if my friends are friends with other people.
4 Friendship Points

• A friend can tell me if she's feeling worried.
2 Friendship Points

• I always remember my friends' birthdays.
2 Friendship Points

• I would help a friend with homework.
2 Friendship Points

• I like to make little gifts for my friends.
2 Friendship Points

• I'd lend a friend my prettiest top.
1 Friendship Point

• I often give my friends compliments.
2 Friendship Points

• My friends describe me as trustworthy.
2 Friendship Points

• I don't talk about friends behind their backs.
3 Friendship Points

• I've never broken a promise to a friend.
4 Friendship Points

• I would give a friend my last sweet.
1 Friendship Point

0–10 Average Friend! The more you put into your friendships, the more you'll get out of them. Why not spend the rest of the day making a gift for a friend?

10–20 Good Friend! Don't be afraid to show your friends how important they are to you.

20+ Best Friend! Your friends adore you and know they can always count on you to be there for them. Keep up the good work!

Decorate the lollipops and draw your own.

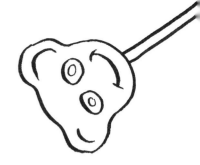

GIRL POWER!

Take inspiration from these incredible girls.

TSUNAMI HERO

While on holiday in Thailand in 2004, Tilly Smith, an 11-year-old from Surrey in England, noticed that the sea was strangely bubbly. Just two weeks before, her class had been learning about giant waves, known as tsunamis, and had watched a film about one that struck in Hawaii, in 1946. She knew these were danger signs.

Tilly said to her mum, 'Seriously, there is definitely going to be a tsunami.' Finally her mum started to listen, and the family took refuge with minutes to spare. That day, Tilly saved the lives of her family and over 100 other people. She received a special award for her quick thinking.

NO STOPPING HER

Born in 1990, surfer Bethany Hamilton, from Hawaii in the USA, could catch a wave by the time she was seven years old. By the age of 13, she had won lots of local surfing competitions and was on her way to becoming a professional.

One terrifying day, Bethany was in the sea with her best friend Alana when they were attacked by a tiger shark. The shark was over 4 metres (13 feet) long and it tore off Bethany's left arm. She lost more than 60% of her blood, but she survived.

Bethany refused to give up her surfing career and was back on her board just 26 days later. In 2005, she came first in the Explorer Women's division of the national championships!

These two girls took their right to an education into their own hands.

SCHOOL FOR ALL

Thandiwe Chama is from Lusaka, in Zambia. When her school was shut down because it had no teachers left, Thandiwe led 60 pupils in a march to find another place to learn. She was just eight years old, but Thandiwe was determined that they should receive an education.

The pupils were taken in by another school, but as there wasn't enough space, they were taught outside in the hot sun. Thandiwe persuaded a local official to pay for a new building.

Since then, Thandiwe has been fighting for a right to education for all children, no matter how poor they may be.

In 2007, she was awarded the International Children's Peace Prize.

PRIZE-WINNING CAMPAIGN

The 2008 winner of the International Children's Peace Prize was Mayra Avellar Neves from Brazil. Mayra grew up in a poor area of Rio de Janeiro – one of the most dangerous cities in the world. When she was 15 years old, the violence in the area where she lived became so bad that all the schools and hospitals closed down.

Bravely, Mayra organized a protest march to draw attention to the problems there. Hundreds of people took part, and, as a result, children were able to return to school. Mayra then organized another march to campaign for fairer treatment of people who live in slums.

INDIAN HEADSCARF DANCE

Namaste! You can use any large scarf or shawl to do this dance routine – just put on some music and get dancing!

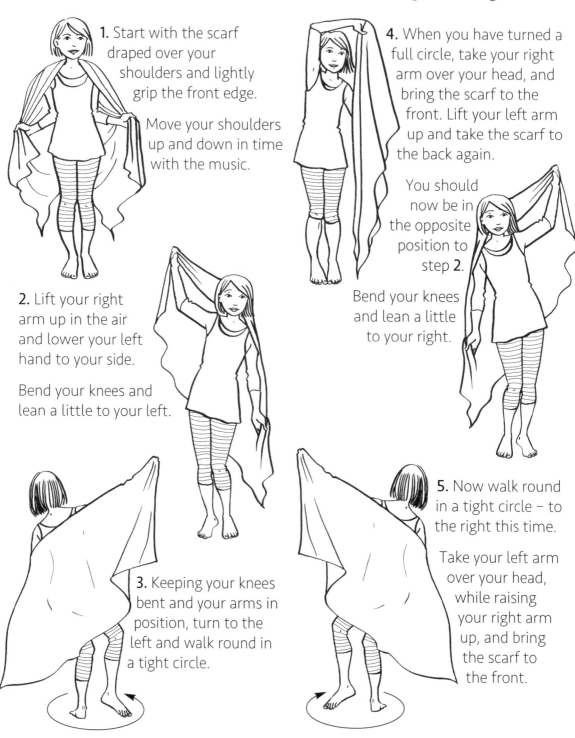

1. Start with the scarf draped over your shoulders and lightly grip the front edge.

Move your shoulders up and down in time with the music.

2. Lift your right arm up in the air and lower your left hand to your side.

Bend your knees and lean a little to your left.

3. Keeping your knees bent and your arms in position, turn to the left and walk round in a tight circle.

4. When you have turned a full circle, take your right arm over your head, and bring the scarf to the front. Lift your left arm up and take the scarf to the back again.

You should now be in the opposite position to step **2.**

Bend your knees and lean a little to your right.

5. Now walk round in a tight circle – to the right this time.

Take your left arm over your head, while raising your right arm up, and bring the scarf to the front.

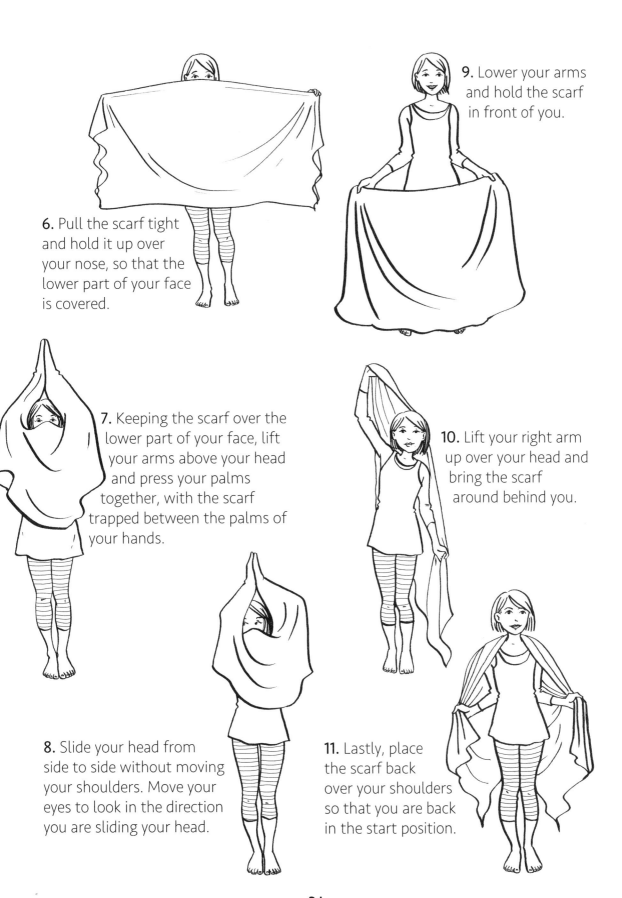

6. Pull the scarf tight and hold it up over your nose, so that the lower part of your face is covered.

9. Lower your arms and hold the scarf in front of you.

7. Keeping the scarf over the lower part of your face, lift your arms above your head and press your palms together, with the scarf trapped between the palms of your hands.

10. Lift your right arm up over your head and bring the scarf around behind you.

8. Slide your head from side to side without moving your shoulders. Move your eyes to look in the direction you are sliding your head.

11. Lastly, place the scarf back over your shoulders so that you are back in the start position.

RAINY DAY SCIENTISTS

Roll up your sleeves and turn your kitchen into a laboratory with these excellent experiments.

SUPER SUGAR ROCKS

In this experiment, you can make your own scientific sugar lolly from a 'supersaturated' solution of sugar.

You will need:

• an empty jam jar, with lid
• a piece of string, 15 cm (6 in) long • a bag of white sugar.

Warning: Always ask an adult to help you when you need to use the kettle.

Sugar is a substance that is soluble in a liquid. This means that when it is added to water, it dissolves. The water becomes sugary, and there are no sugar granules left. The liquid is now a solution. There's a limit to how much sugar can be dissolved in a glass of water though, and when this limit is reached, the solution is saturated.

However, there's something you can do to get more sugar into a solution: add heat.

To see this in action, ask an adult to help you boil the kettle, then fill your jam jar with hot water. The jar will be hot, so ask the adult to hold it steady for you with a cloth or an oven glove.

Now it's time to add the sugar. See if you can guess how many teaspoons of sugar will dissolve in the hot water. Add a spoonful at a time, and stir until it dissolves.

When no more sugar will dissolve, lower your piece of string into the water, so that the end hangs over the rim of the jar. Trap it with the jar lid, and leave the jar in a safe place.

As the solution cools, the extra sugar will not be able to stay dissolved, and sugar crystals will start to form on the string.

After a week, you will have a delicious sugar lolly! Yum.

SHE'S ELECTRIC!

Use this experiment to create your own static electricity.

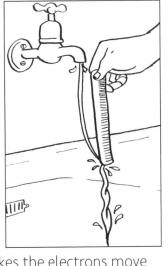

You will need:

• a plastic comb • running water.

Everything in the world is made atoms – tiny particles that are too small to see. Inside each atom, there are even smaller particles: protons, neutrons and electrons. Protons have a positive electrical charge. Neutrons are neutral – they have no charge. Electrons are negatively charged.

Most of the time, atoms have no charge. However, if you rub two objects together, you can create a charge that makes the electrons move from one atom to another. This charge is static electricity.

To do this yourself, simply run your comb through your hair a few times. This will make negatively charged electrons jump from your hair to the comb. The comb will now have a negative charge.

Now run a very thin stream of water and hold the charged comb close to it. The water will be attracted to the comb and 'bend' towards it!

SOAP-TASTIC!

Discover how gas expands when heated with this incredible experiment.

Warning: Make sure you ask an adult for help with the microwave in this experiment.

You will need:

• a bar of soap • a microwave
• a microwaveable bowl.

Note. A bar of soap that has lots of tiny air bubbles in it – one that floats in the bath, for example – will work best for this experiment.

Remove any stickers from the soap and place it in the bowl in the microwave. Heat for two minutes on full power, watching all the time to see what happens. As the soap gets hotter, the gas inside the bubbles – air – expands and the solid bar of soap will foam up out of the bowl. Amazing!

Allow the soap to cool for at least five minutes before you touch it. Clean the microwave before anyone cooks food in it.

SLEEPOVER PUZZLER

The girls are having a sleepover, so grab a pen and test your skills in these chums' challenges! You'll find the answers on page 63. First, can you find your way through the maze to get to the sleepover on time? On the way, you need to pick up your friends Katie and Jessie.

Katie

SLEEPOVER MYSTERY MAZE

Jessie

DRESSING-GOWN DILEMMA

Can you work out which dressing gown belongs to which girl?

A	B	C	D
Jenny	Jo	Kim	Katie

SNACK TIME!

The girls are having pizza for their midnight feast. Two of them have chosen identical slices – can you spot which two are identical?

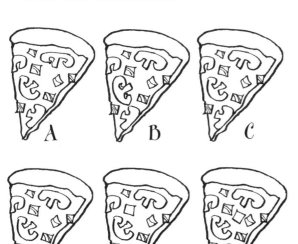

A   B   C

D   E   F

MIDDLE-NAME LOGIC

The girls are trying to guess each other's middle names. Can you give them a helping hand? Write the correct first name next to the middle names below, using the following clues:

1. Jenny's middle name starts with an S.

2. Jo's middle name has an L in it.

3. Kim's middle name is not the longest.

4. Katie's name is as long as Jenny's.

. . . . Isabelle

. . . . Coral

. . . . Sophie

. . . . Sarah

HOPPING ORIGAMI

Make an origami frog that really hops! You can then use it as a counter for the lily-pad game on the next page. All you need is a square of froggy green paper.

1. First, fold the piece of paper in half.

the two sides together so that they meet in the middle.

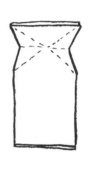 

2. Fold the top-left corner down, so that the top of the paper lines up with the right-hand side. Then unfold it again.

The top of the paper will now fold down to form a triangle, like this:

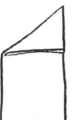

3. Now fold the top-right corner down, so that the top of the paper lines up with the left-hand side. Then unfold it again.

6. Fold the bottom of the paper up so that the edge lines up with the bottom of the triangle.

4. Turn the paper over and fold down the top at the point where the diagonal creases meet, to make a horizontal crease, as shown here.

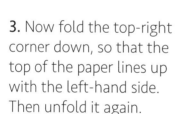

7. Fold the corners at the bottom of the triangle up to make the frog's front legs.

5. Unfold the paper again and hold it by the edges of the horizontal line. Bring

8. Next, fold in the straight sides, so that they meet in the middle.

9. Fold the straight sides up, so that they reach the bottom of the frog's legs. Unfold them again, leaving a crease.

10. Reach under the flaps at the bottom with your thumbs, holding the middle in place with your fingers. Pull the flaps upwards and outwards into points, so that the lower edge comes up to reach the bottom of the frog's legs.

11. Fold the points down, so that they meet at the bottom, as shown here.

12. Now fold these points out diagonally to make your frog's back legs.

13. Next, fold your frog in half across the middle, then fold the back legs back again in a zigzag, so that the frog's back legs will be underneath its body.

14. That's it! Turn your frog over. To make it hop, press and flick on its back. You can use your frog for a game of Lily-Pad Hoppers on the next page.

Note: If you would like to make frog counters to play Lily-Pad Hoppers (see page 38), start with a square of paper measuring roughly 10 cm (4 in) across. Use a different shade for each player.

LILY-PAD HOPPERS

Race your friends across the pond and be the first to make it to the riverbank on the other side!

First, get each of your friends to make an origami frog as a counter (see pages 36 and 37). Alternatively, use a different coin each instead. Place the frogs at the start, then take turns to spin the spinner (follow the instructions opposite to get spinning) and move forward the number of spaces shown.

You stop to look at some tadpoles. Miss a turn.

Take a shortcut across the stepping stones.

START HERE

A gnome points you in the wrong direction. Move back 3 spaces.

Slide down the swan's neck to move on 2 spaces.

Miss a turn while you feed the fish.

You get a boost from a snack of flies – move on 1 space.

SPINNER

Cut around the dotted line and pierce the middle of your spinner with a toothpick.

To take a spin, hold the toothpick upright on the playing surface and spin it between your thumb and forefinger. When the spinning stops, the number at the top is the number of lily pads your frog is allowed to hop.

You catch a lift on a dragonfly. Move forward 3 spaces.

Take a shortcut down the waterfall.

A duck steals your breakfast. Miss a turn.

GOOD HOPPING!

FINISH HERE

You stop to make a crown of lilies. Miss a turn.

Everyone else's lily pads sink – they all miss a turn!

Your feet get tangled in reeds. Move back 3 spaces.

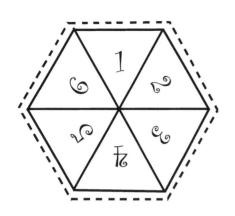

Fill the page with rainbows and pretty birds.

MAJOR MIX-UP

The pieces of this jigsaw have got mixed up with some pieces from
another jigsaw. Can you work out which three pieces fit in the gaps?
The answers are on page 63.

WET WEATHER WISHES

When the weather outside is frightful, it's time to decide whether you'd rather splash around in puddles or curl up with a good book.

If it is raining outside, I am more likely to ...

... be happy – I love the rain! ☐

... hope for a rainbow. ☐

... feel miserable. ☐

... have fun indoors. ☐

The last thing I want to do when it rains is ...

... let it change my plans. ☐

... go outside. ☐

... get wet feet. ☐

... stay at home. ☐

The best thing to do if I am out in the rain is ...

... splash in the puddles! ☐

... drink raindrops. ☐

... spin my umbrella. ☐

... have a water fight. ☐

When the weather is wet, I'd rather be ...

... shopping with my friends. ☐

... playing in the park. ☐

... riding my bike. ☐

... reading in the sun. ☐

If it's raining, my parents are most likely to say ...

... 'It's good for the plants.' ☐

... 'Do some homework.' ☐

... 'Help me around the house.' ☐

... 'Play outside anyway.' ☐

On a rainy day, the best thing to do indoors is ...

... imagine I'm somewhere hot. ☐

... play with my brother or sister. ☐

... watch a DVD. ☐

... curl up with a good book. ☐

FLOWER POWER

There are so many things to do on a rainy day that it can be hard to choose how to spend your time. Use some flower power to help you decide!

1. First, write an indoor activity that you enjoy in each of the flower petals below.

2. Count the number of letters in your first name, and add it to the number of letters in your surname.

3. Divide this number by two. If you end up with a half number, round it up. (For example, if you get 5.5, round it up to 6.)

4. Starting at the top petal, count round the flower petals until you reach your number, then shade in that petal.

5. Continue counting on the following unshaded petals, skipping any that are already shaded in. Every time your reach your number, shade in that petal.

6. When there is only one petal left, do that activity!

AMAZING ANIMAL FACTS

One of these Amazing Animal Facts is false – can you spot which one?
All will be revealed on page 63!

1. TASTY FEET?

Some butterflies have special sensors on their feet that allow them to taste things as they walk over them. This ability is not usually used to taste food but to find good places to lay eggs.

2. SEE-THROUGH OR SO UNTRUE?

Some scientists believe that polar bears have transparent fur that only looks white because it reflects light.

3. POINTY BUT POSSIBLE?

Rhino horns are made from the same substance as human fingernails.

4. HOW 'EGGS'-ELLENT?

Hummingbirds lay the smallest eggs of any bird, as tiny as 7 mm (¼ in) long!

5. STRANGE SNACK?

There is a type of Asian moth that has evolved to feed on the tears of buffaloes.

6. ELE-FANTASTICAL?

Elephant pregnancies last for nine months, just like human pregnancies.

TREASURE HUNT

Take part in a treasure hunt that will have you racing all over the park!

This treasure hunt works using numbers and letters called co-ordinates.
To use each co-ordinate clue, place your finger on the letter given. Move along the row to the column that matches the number. In that square you will find a new co-ordinate clue. Keep following the clues and finding the co-ordinates until you land in a square with a symbol instead of a co-ordinate. Use the key at the bottom to work out where the treasure is hidden, then turn to page 63 to check your answer. The first clue for the treasure hunt is at E3.

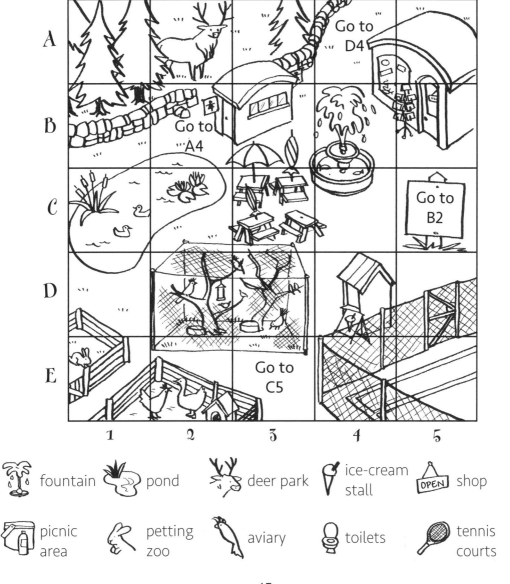

IT'S A BIRDIE!

This little bird makes such a cute present that
you might want to give it to yourself!

You will need:

• a pencil • a piece of paper • a sharp pair of scissors • a piece of fabric about the
size of this page (try to choose a fabric that doesn't fray easily, such as felt)
• pins • a needle and thread • 2 buttons • a pair of old socks.

What to do:

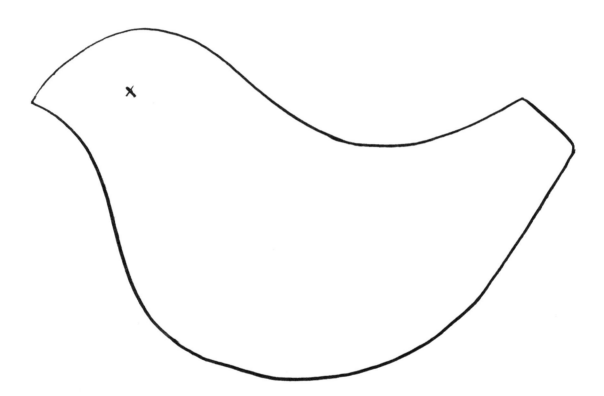

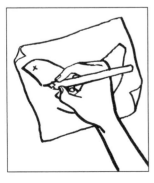

1. Trace over the picture of a bird, above, and cut it out. This is your template.

2. Fold the large piece of fabric in

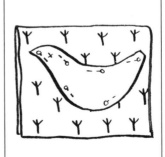

half with the printed side on the outside, if patterned.

3. Pin the paper bird on to the fabric, as shown here.

4. Carefully cut around the edge of the paper bird so that you end up with two matching fabric birds. Unpin the template.

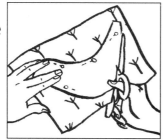

5. It's now time to sew some button eyes on to the fabric birds. Take a piece of thread the length of your arm and thread the needle. Pull the thread halfway through, then tie the ends in a double knot.

6. Place one of the buttons on the printed side of one of the fabric birds where its eye would be (marked with an X opposite).

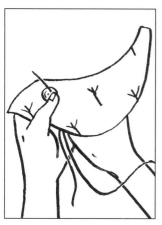

7. From below, push the needle up through the fabric and through one of the holes in the button. Pull it all the way through until the knot hits the fabric.

8. Push the needle down into the next hole and continue passing the needle up and down through the fabric and buttonholes until the button is secure.

9. Finish with the needle on the non-printed side of the fabric and secure it with a double knot. Trim the thread.

10. Sew the second button on to the other bird-shaped piece of fabric in the same way.

11. Pin the two bird-shaped pieces of fabric together so the printed-sides face outwards.

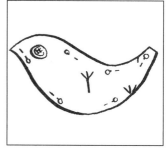

12. Thread the needle with another piece of thread about the length of your arm. Push the needle through the fabric about ½ cm (¼ in) from the edge.

13. Bring the needle back up through the fabric about 2 mm (⅛ in) to the right of the first hole. Make several stitches on this spot to secure the thread.

14. Push the needle up and down through the fabric, making stitches that are 2 mm (⅛ in) long.

15. Continue sewing around the bird until just a 2 cm (¾ in) hole is left.

16. Cut the socks into pieces, then push the pieces through the hole to stuff the bird.

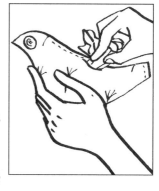

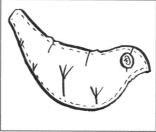

17. Sew the hole closed, then tie the end of the thread in a knot and cut off the excess.

Top Tip. Why not add a loop of ribbon, so that you can hang your birdie up?

BRAIN-BASHERS

See how quickly you can complete these logical puzzles without your brain exploding! Record how long it takes you to work out each one in the spaces provided. You'll find the answers on pages 63 and 64.

TROPHY TIME

Three friends, Emily, Alyssa and Preeya, are discussing how many football trophies a boy in their class, named Alex, has won. Only one of them is correct – the other two are wrong. Can you work out who by studying their conversation?

'Alex is so sweet, and he's won more than one football trophy,' said Emily.

'He's won at least five!' Alyssa scoffed.

Preeya interrupted, saying, 'I heard that it's an even number.'

How many trophies has Alex won?

Time: . . . .

SUNFLOWER SUMS

Alice is growing a sunflower that doubles in height every day. After 30 days, the sunflower will be as tall as she is. After how many days would the sunflower be half her height?

Time: . . . .

SUMMER FUN

Summer's mum has four children. The first child is called April, the second child is called May, and the third child is called June. What is the name of the fourth child?

Time: . . . .

DONKEY DILEMMA

Can you move just one toothpick to make the donkey change position?

Time: . . . .

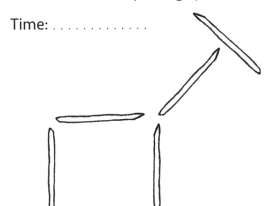

CHOCOLATE CONUNDRUM

Rebecca has bought three boxes of chocolates for her friends: white chocolates for Kate, milk chocolates for Sarah, and a mixture of milk and white chocolates for Bella. However, the chocolate labels have been mixed up, and the boxes all look the same! None of the labels are correct.

Rebecca thinks she can shake a chocolate out of one box without tearing it, but how could she work out which label goes on which box by taking just one chocolate from one box?

Time: . . . .

WHO'S THE TOP?

Four friends are trying to decide who is the tallest – can you work it out just from these clues?

Louisa is only taller than Siân and Preeya is shorter than Sally. However, Preeya is taller than Siân, and Sally is taller than Louisa.

How tall are they? Tick one box for each of them.

Time: . . . .

	100 cm (3 ft 3 in)	105 cm (3 ft 5 in)	110 cm (3 ft 7 in)	115 cm (3 ft 9 in)
Louisa				
Siân				
Sally				
Preeya				

HELLO, HANJIE!

Konnichiwa! (That's 'hello' in Japanese.) Hanjie is a brain-boggling Japanese puzzle that's perfect for *tsuyu* – the rainy season. See how quickly you can complete these challenges, then turn to page 64 for the answers.

Shade in squares in these puzzles to reveal the hidden images. The numbers at the end of each row and column reveal the number of shaded squares that appear together in that row or column, in order, from left to right or from the top down.

For example, the clue '1, 1' tells you that you need to shade in a single square, then leave a gap of at least one square before shading in another single square somewhere in that row.

Novice

Get started with this easy-peasy puzzle for beginners. Look at the numbers along the top of the grid – do you notice that one column should have all five squares filled? Start there, and you should soon find the spaces filling up!

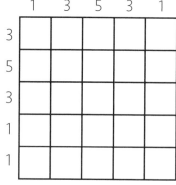

	1	3	5	3	1
3					
5					
3					
1					
1					

Expert

This one is slightly trickier, so some of the squares have been filled in for you. Remember, if there is more than one group of shaded squares in a row or column, there must be a gap of at least one square between them.

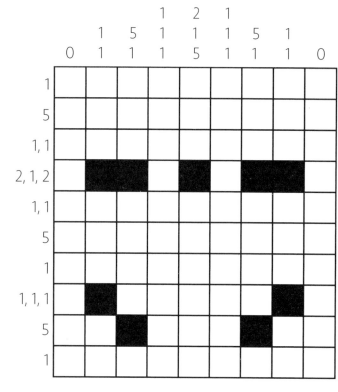

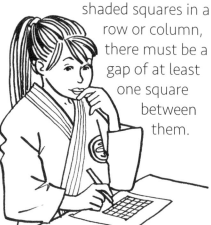

FUTURE FANTASTIC!

What will your future look like? Peer into a crystal ball and make your predictions! It's said that if you write your goals down you're more likely to achieve them, so get started on making your dream future a reality!

In ten years time I will be a _____.

I will be living in _____ with _____.

My greatest achievement will be _____

_____.

I will be on my way to becoming a _____

_____.

My best friend will be _____ and

the thing we will most enjoy doing will be

_____.

A RAINY DAY ADVENTURE

Maria pressed her face up against the window and looked out miserably.

It had been raining for twelve days in a row, and she was bored, bored, bored.

'Come here, Maria,' said her grandmother. 'I have something to tell you that I think will cheer you up.'

Maria brightened, glad of anything that might be interesting.

A grandmother's wisdom

'You might be bored now, Maria, but there will be a full moon tonight. Did you know that if you look into a puddle at midnight, you will see your future in the light cast by a full moon?'

Now that didn't sound boring at all! That sounded like exactly the kind of adventure Maria had been dreaming about ever since it had started raining.

Maria called her friend Amelie at once, and they hatched a plan. Half an hour later, Amelie was standing on Maria's doorstep in her mackintosh and wellington boots, ringing the doorbell.

Maria pulled her friend into the house. 'I've set the alarm clock for 11.30 p.m.,' Maria informed her excitedly, 'and I've prepared a midnight feast for us to snack on before we head out to discover our future.'

Amelie looked at Maria and raised one eyebrow. 'It's going to be a fun adventure, but you don't believe that rubbish do you?'

'We'll see,' replied Maria, with a knowing smile. Her grandmother had never been wrong about anything like this before.

The girls got ready for bed and spent at least an hour whispering and giggling before sleep finally took hold of them and they drifted off.

Brrrring, brrrring, brrrring!

The alarm brought the girls awake, and they jumped out of bed and tucked into the feast that Maria had prepared.

When they were full, Maria and Amelie pulled waterproofs on over their nightclothes and headed out into the pouring rain.

'Come on,' said Maria, taking hold of her friend's hand and pulling her into the garden. 'The water always pools over here, so there will be a perfect puddle for us to look into.'

As they stood over the puddle, the rain clouds parted, and the full moon shone through, illuminating the girls in an eerie white light. They held on tight to each other's hands and cautiously peered down into the puddle.

A mysterious reflection

Looking up out of the puddle they saw two smiling ladies, who were also holding hands, peering back at them. The girls stared in shocked silence as one of the ladies started to speak.

'Oh, my dears, you're so young!'

She turned to look at her friend, saying, 'Remember when that was us, peering into this puddle?' Her friend nodded.

'I didn't believe it was going to work, but it did. We discovered our future. We discovered that it would be full of fun and laughter and all the wonderful things that make up life.'

'And the most important thing we learned was that we would be there for each other through all of it – that we would be friends forever – even when we were much, much older.'

'But who are you both?' cried Maria.

'Dear girls, we're you, of course! This is your future.'

Always there

Maria and Amelie laughed and cried and hugged each other. 'Friends forever!' they declared in unison!

JEAN GENIUS

Here's how to turn an
ordinary exercise book into
a stylish denim notebook.

You will need:

• an old pair of jeans (check with an adult that it's okay for you
to use them) • a pair of scissors • a blank exercise book • a pen
• strong, all-purpose adhesive • roughly 1 m (3 ft) of wide ribbon.

What you do:

1. First cut the legs off the jeans, so that you have two tubes of fabric. Then cut along the inside seams of one of the legs, so that you have a piece of denim with a seam down the centre.

2. Lay the denim flat on a table with the wrong side facing up. Open out the book on top of the piece of fabric, so that the seam runs horizontally across the middle of the cover. Use the pen to draw around it.

3. Draw another rectangle about 3 cm (1¼ in) larger around the one you've just drawn, then cut along this outside line.

4. Cover the front of the book with glue, then stick the fabric to it, matching up the edges of the book with the inner rectangle drawn on the fabric. Repeat for the back cover.

5. Cut a diagonal line across the corners, and in the middle at the top and bottom of the fabric, as shown below.

6. Spread a thin line of glue around the three outer edges of the inside front cover of the book. Then fold the edges of the fabric in and stick them down.

Repeat for the back cover.

7. Cut your length of ribbon in half and add a dab of glue to the end of one piece. Stick it to the inside edge of the front cover. Repeat for the back cover and leave to dry.

Top tip. If your length of ribbon has a wrong side and a right side, glue the right side to the inside covers, so that it shows when you close your note book.

8. Cut carefully around one of the back pockets of your jeans. You should now have a denim pocket with two layers of fabric. Cover the back of the pocket with glue, then stick it to the front of your notebook. Leave to dry.

In-jean-ious!

Decorate her coat and boots.

HEADSCARF HEAVEN

Rainy weather can play havoc with your hairdo, so wrap up in a headscarf to keep your locks looking perfect!

CLASSIC WRAP

1. Take a large square headscarf and fold it in half along the diagonal to create a triangle.

2. Place it over your head so that the middle of the folded side is in the centre of your forehead and the tip is pointing down your back.

3. Take the two ends and tie them in a knot at the back of your head under your hair.

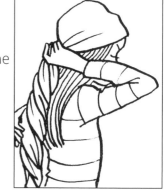

GYPSY CHIC

1. Hold a sarong over your head so that the middle of one of the long sides is flat against your forehead.

2. Gather the sarong at the nape of your neck, then twist it around all the way to the bottom.

3. Tie a knot in the sarong at the nape of your neck, then pull the length of it forward over your shoulder.

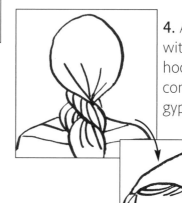

4. Accessorize with some large hoop earrings to complete the gypsy look.

4. Push the front of the headscarf back above your hairline for a softer look.

ARABIAN DREAM

1. Tip your head forward and hold a sarong over your head so that the middle of one of the long sides is flat against the nape of your neck.

2. Gather the fabric at your forehead and twist it all the way to the bottom.

3. Lift your head up and take the twisted fabric back over your head and around one side. Then pull it forward over the opposite shoulder.

4. Accessorize with lots of sparkly bangles.

VINTAGE QUEEN

1. Take a square headscarf and fold it in half to create a triangle.

2. Hold the headscarf across your shoulders so that the tip is pointing down your back and the straight edge is underneath your hair.

3. Pick up the two ends and tie them in a knot on top of your head.

4. Pull the point of the scarf up over your head, tucking long hair away inside, then slip the end of the scarf under the front of the knot.

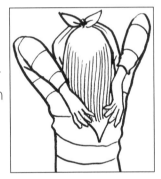

5. Tie the ends in a second knot to ensure the point stays in place, then tuck the ends in too.

6. Wear with a stripy sailor top to complete the look.

THEATRELAND!

It's premiere night at the theatre – are you red-carpet ready?
The answers are on page 64.

Which photo has been taken by which person as the actors walk the red carpet?
Think about the way the cameras are pointing to help you work out your answers.

WHO'S THE LEADING LADY?

Can you spot ten differences between the female lead and her stunt double?

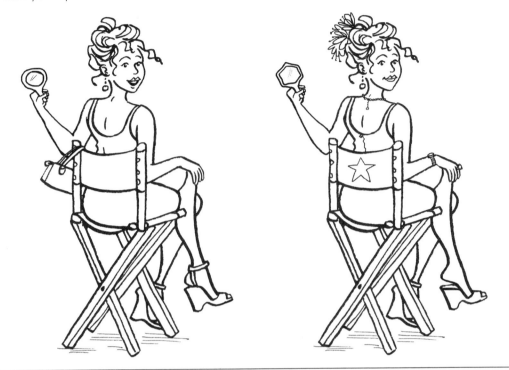

AUTOGRAPH HUNTER

Can you find your way backstage to get an autograph from the lead actor?

59

TOP THAT!

Make a set of personalized *Top That!* cards to play with your friends or to give to someone as a special gift.

You will need:

• 2 pieces of thin A4 (8 ½ x 11 in) card • scissors • old magazines with lots of photos of celebrities • a glue stick • a black pen • transparent sticky-back plastic (optional).

1. Fold each piece of card into thirds across the width, then cut along the lines to get six short strips of card.

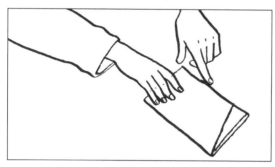

2. Fold each strip of card into thirds to make playing-card sized rectangles. Cut along the folds so that you have 18 small cards.

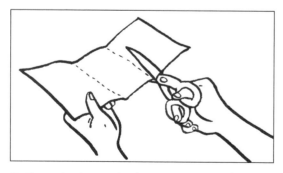

3. Search through the magazines for photos of actors and singers that you like. Look for pictures where the heads are roughly 3 cm (1 in) high. You'll need pictures of 18 different people altogether.

4. When you have chosen your magazine pictures, cut around each person's head. Glue each of the heads at the top of a card, leaving space underneath to write.

5. Now choose five categories to rate each celebrity on. For example, you might pick: dress sense, singing skills, acting ability, hair style and kindness to fans – or pick your own categories.

Dress sense: · · · · · · · · ·
Singing skills: · · · · · · · ·
Acting ability: · · · · · · · ·
Hair style: · · · · · · · · · ·
Kindness to fans: · · · · · ·

Score each person out of 10 in each of the categories to complete the cards.

Top Tip. Make sure that you include at least one high score and at least one low score on each card.

6. For a long-lasting finish, cover your cards in transparent sticky-back plastic.

HOW TO PLAY

Any number of people can play *Top That!* Deal the cards face down. Each player then takes their top card and the player to the left of the dealer reads out one of their categories and the score, for example:

'Singing skills: 8.'

The other players then read out the same category, and the player with the highest value wins all the cards from that round.

That player then puts the card to the bottom of her pile, and picks a category to play from the card on the top.

If two or more players share the top score for a category, all the cards from that round are placed in the middle and the same player chooses another category from her next card. The winner of the round wins all the cards from the middle as well as the cards in play.

The player with all the cards at the end is the winner.

SPOT THAT DIFFERENCE!

There are five differences between the two pictures of the girl playing Top That! Can you spot them all? You'll find the answers on page 64.

ALL THE ANSWERS

RODEO ROUNDUP
pages 8 and 9

Round 'Em Up!
Sarah-Jane has lassoed a bull.
Jessie has lassoed a pony.
Lucie has lassoed a goat.
Emmie has lassoed a calf.
Katie has lassoed a prairie dog.

Most Wanted
Sarah-Jane is on the run.

Lassosudoku

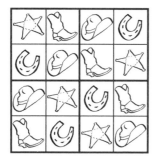

Wagon Bull Run

PUPPY POWER!
page 13

Puppy **A** belongs to Rosie.
Puppy **B** belongs to Leila.
Puppy **C** belongs to Caitlin.

DANCE AROUND THE WORLD
page 14

A is Spain.	**E** is China.
B is France.	**F** is Ghana.
C is India.	**G** is Brazil.
D is Egypt.	**H** is USA.

HAWAIIAN LUAU
pages 22 and 23

Party Invitation
The party is at the Halona Blowhole.

Sudoku Hawaiian-Style

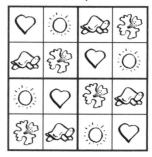

Luscious Luau Smoothies
Smoothie **A** is yours.

Paradise Divide

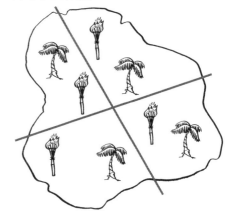

SLEEPOVER PUZZLER
pages 34 and 35

Sleepover Mystery Maze

Dressing-Gown Dilemma
Dressing gown **C** belongs to Jenny.
Dressing gown **D** belongs to Jo.
Dressing gown **A** belongs to Kim.
Dressing gown **B** belongs to Katie.

Snack Time!
C and D are the matching pizza slices.

Middle-Name Logic
Jo's middle name is Isabelle.
Katie's middle name is Coral.
Kim's middle name is Sophie.
Jenny's middle name is Sarah.

MAJOR MIX-UP
page 41

The missing pieces of the jigsaw puzzle
are **B**, **C** and **E**.

ANIMAL FACTS
page 44

The false fact is number **6**. Elephant
pregnancies are in fact on average
22 months long – more than twice as
long as human pregnancies!

TREASURE HUNT
page 45

The treasure is in the ice-cream stall.

BRAIN-BASHERS
pages 48 and 49

Trophy Time
Alex has three trophies. Here's why:
If Alex had won 'at least five' trophies,
then Alyssa and Emily would both be
right as that is 'more than one'. If he
had won an even number of trophies, as
Preeya says, Emily would also be right as
that is always more than one. Emily's is
the only answer that can be right when
the other girls' answers are wrong.

Sunflower Sums
Because the sunflower doubles in height
every day, and is as tall as her after 30
days, it will be half her height the day
before, after 29 days.

Summer Fun
The fourth child is Summer!

Donkey Dilemma

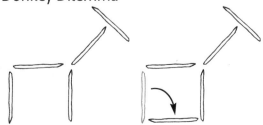

Chocolate Conundrum

If Rebecca removes a chocolate from the box marked 'Milk and White Chocolate', the solution is simple.

All of the labels are wrong, so the box marked 'Milk and White Chocolate' must contain either milk or white chocolate. If Rebecca gets a milk chocolate, then that box must contain only milk chocolates. This means that the box that is marked 'White Chocolate' must be the mixed box and the remaining box should have the 'White Chocolate' label.

Who's the top?

Louisa is 105 cm (3 ft 5 in) tall.
Siân 100 cm (3 ft 3 in) tall.
Sally 115 cm (3 ft 9 in) tall.
Preeya 110 cm (3 ft 7 in) tall.

HELLO, HANJIE!

page 50

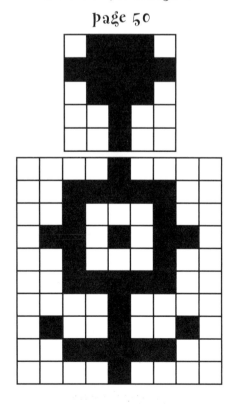

THEATRELAND

pages 58 and 59

Photo **A** was taken by photographer **6**.
Photo **B** was taken by photographer **3**.
Photo **C** was taken by photographer **4**.
Photo **D** was taken by photographer **1**.
Photo **E** was taken by photographer **5**.
Photo **F** was taken by photographer **2**.

Who's The Leading Lady?

Autograph Hunter

SPOT THAT DIFFERENCE!

page 61

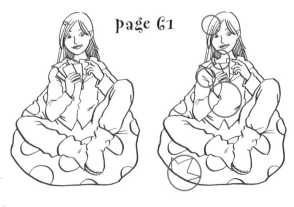